THE BLACK AMERICAN JOURNEY

JUNETEENTH

"The fact is none of us are free
till we're all free."
⌒ Opal Lee ⌒
Activist and Texas resident
June 18, 2020

BY EMILY DOLBEAR

Published by The Child's World®
1980 Lookout Drive, Mankato, MN 56003-1705
800-599-READ • www.childsworld.com

PHOTOS

Cover and page 4: Kate Kultsevych/Shutterstock.com
Interior: Antwon McMullen/Shutterstock.com: 27, 31; Dylan Buell/Getty Images for
VIBE: 23; Everett Collection/Shutterstock.com: 9, 14, 28; Fiora Watts/Shutterstock.
com: 25; fitzcrittle/Shutterstock.com: 26, 29 (right); G.H. Houghton/Library of
Congress, Prints and Photographs Division: 5; G.M. Stephenson/Austin History
Center, Austin Public Library: 20, 29 (left); Hubbard & Mix/Library of Congress,
Prints and Photographs Division: 13; Lee Russell/Library of Congress, Prints and
Photographs Division: 22; Library of Congress, Prints and Photographs Division: 8,
10, 12; North Wind Picture Archives: 6, 7, 15, 18; Paul Moseley/Star-Telegram via AP:
24; Sam A. Cooley/Library of Congress, Prints and Photographs Division: 17; Sam A.
Cooley/The Miriam and Ira D. Wallach Division of Art, Prints and Photographs/The
New York Public Library: 19; US National Archives and Records Administration: 11

LIBRARY OF CONGRESS CATALOGING-IN-PUBLICATION DATA

ISBN 9781503853799 (Reinforced Library Binding)
ISBN 9781503854017 (Portable Document Format)
ISBN 9781503854130 (Online Multi-user eBook)
LCCN: 2020943579

Printed in the United States of America

Cover and page 4 caption:
Juneteenth is a day of
celebration and remembrance
for many Americans.

CONTENTS

Chapter One

A COUNTRY DIVIDED

In the early 1860s, the northern and southern United States fought each other in the U.S. Civil War. The issue of slavery had divided them for many years. The northern states had **abolished** slavery. The South depended on enslaved people to run its large plantations, or farms. Many people in the North opposed the spread of slavery to the western states. Many people in the South supported slavery in the new territories.

An enslaved family on a Virginia plantation in 1862.

In early 1861, seven Southern states left the United States to form their own government. They were South Carolina, Mississippi, Florida, Alabama, Georgia, Louisiana, and Texas. The states of Virginia, Arkansas, Tennessee, and North Carolina joined later. These eleven slave states called themselves the Confederate States of America. The Northern states that remained were known as the Union.

The U.S. Civil War began in Charleston, South Carolina. Early in the morning on April 12, 1861, Confederate forces attacked the Union's Fort Sumter. They captured it the next day. The war continued for almost four years. Confederate general Robert E. Lee surrendered at Appomattox Court House in Virginia on April 9, 1865. The war remains the deadliest in U.S. history. More than 600,000 soldiers lost their lives.

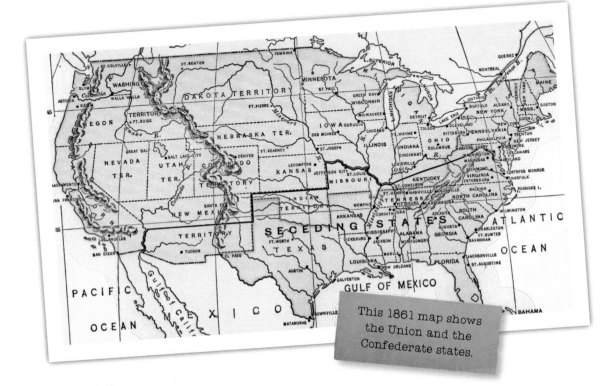

This 1861 map shows the Union and the Confederate states.

The end of the U.S. Civil War didn't put an end to slavery right away. More than two years earlier, President Abraham Lincoln had written the Emancipation Proclamation. This document freed enslaved people in the Confederate states, as of January 1, 1863.

"I never, in my life, felt more certain that I was doing right than I do in signing this paper," Lincoln said. "If my name goes into history, it will be for this act, and my whole soul is in it." The Emancipation Proclamation also opened the military to freed African Americans. Nearly 200,000 of them fought to help the North win the war.

The all-Black 54th Massachusetts Regiment fought for the Union at Fort Wagner, South Carolina, in 1863.

Lawmakers voted to design a new Mississippi flag in 2020. Designs will have no Confederate battle symbol and include the words "In God We Trust."

But the Confederate states ignored the Emancipation Proclamation. The practice of slavery continued there, as well as in the border states. Almost four million African Americans remained enslaved.

Then, on January 31, 1865, Congress proposed a change, or amendment, to the U.S. Constitution forever outlawing slavery. "Neither slavery nor **involuntary servitude**," the text reads, "shall exist within the United States." But the states did not agree to formally approve the Thirteenth Amendment until the end of 1865. President Lincoln, shot by a slavery supporter, died before that historic achievement.

With the Confederate surrender on April 9, 1865, the Union could at last carry out Lincoln's Emancipation Proclamation. But in some places, this was difficult. Fighting continued in Louisiana and Texas.

The last Confederate soldiers put down their arms on June 2, 1865. Their leader, Edmund Kirby-Smith, surrendered his troops at Galveston, Texas. A Union general named Gordon Granger and his troops were on their way to the port city. Freedom for enslaved Americans had been delayed long enough.

Abraham Lincoln was president from 1861 to 1865.

Chapter Two

JUNE 19, 1865

On the morning of June 19, 1865, General Granger arrived by boat in Galveston, Texas. His troops numbered 1,800. The Union general had come to restore order to the region. He also had important news to deliver to the enslaved people of Texas.

Information traveled slowly back then. It moved especially slowly to Texas, thousands of miles southwest of Washington, DC. General Granger's news came as a military order. It was known as General Order Number 3. Many enslaved workers needed someone to read the order to them. This was because many states barred the education of enslaved people.

A Union soldier (in uniform) with formerly enslaved people in South Carolina.

The original order that inspired Juneteenth still exists. The National Archives in Washington, DC, made the first digital copy on June 18, 2020. That is almost exactly 155 years after it was first read.

General Granger read his two-page order to the public more than once. The first time was at the Osterman Building. This was the headquarters of the Union army in Galveston. General Granger then shared the news at the county courthouse. Some historians say he made the announcement again from the balcony of Ashton Villa. Enslaved workers built this elegant brick home in 1859. At one time, it had served as an office for the Confederate army.

"The people of Texas," General Granger read out, "are informed that, in accordance with a proclamation from [the U.S. president], all slaves are free." He continued, "This involves an absolute equality of personal rights and rights of property." The order finally announced "former masters and slaves" were now "employer and hired labor."

General Gordon Granger

General Granger's handwritten Order Number 3 spanned two pages.

General Order Number 3 was posted throughout Galveston. It was printed in newspapers in the city and around the state. The news took time to reach outlying plantations.

The response of those who learned of their freedom that day in Galveston was shock and joy. They cried out. They danced and beat pots. Some wept. Men tossed their hats in the air. As free people, they were able to rejoice freely. "We was all walkin' on golden clouds," a formerly enslaved Texan recalled. "Everybody went wild. . . . We was free. Just like that we was free."

General Granger likely read his order at the local Black church. This house of worship, later called Reedy Chapel Church, was the first place the newly freed people gathered. They celebrated there the answer to a prayer.

People in Richmond, Virginia, walking to celebrate Emancipation Day.

In the 1850s, a group of African Americans escaped to northern Mexico from slavery in the United States. They were called the Mascogos. Their descendants celebrate Juneteenth.

Today, people celebrate June 19 as the holiday Juneteenth. The word comes from *June* and *Nineteenth*. Some people have called it Emancipation Day. Others call it Freedom Day.

A **descendant** of enslaved Texans shared his understanding of Juneteenth. "The way it was explained to me," he said, "19th of June wasn't the exact day the [enslaved person] was freed, but that's the day they told them that they was free." Perhaps that is why many African Americans call it Black Independence Day.

Chapter Three

NEWFOUND FREEDOM

Formerly enslaved people faced huge challenges. They started new lives without political or **economic equality**. They often left plantations with nothing more than the clothing on their backs. Many had been separated from their families when they were enslaved. They had no land, homes, or way to earn a living. They had been denied education. Feeding themselves and their families was a daily struggle.

Formerly enslaved women who continued to live and raise their children on a South Carolina plantation.

Newly freed Americans in Richmond, Virginia, after the city's fall to Union troops in 1865.

Harvesting sugarcane was backbreaking work.

Racial discrimination endured after the U.S. Civil War. In 1865, Southern states began to pass laws called Black codes. Those laws carried on many of the conditions of slavery. They kept formerly enslaved people from voting, owning land, moving, and working freely. One law required any Black person to pay a yearly $100 tax unless they worked on a farm or in a house.

In Texas, some plantation owners never told their enslaved workers about their freedom. The workers continued to harvest cotton, corn, and sugarcane for their enslavers without pay. Weeks or months passed. Freedom for those Texans sometimes required the arrival of a U.S. agent.

Starting in 1865, the U.S. government provided aid through the Freedmen's Bureau. This national agency offered food and clothing to formerly enslaved people, or freedmen and freedwomen. It helped locate lost family members and set up work agreements. The agency, working with freedmen, opened thousands of schools in the South before losing funding in 1870.

When Union general Granger came to Galveston, Texas, on June 19, 1865, nearly 250,000 enslaved people lived in the state.

Freed Texans held their first emancipation celebration on January 1, 1866. It was about six months after General Granger's "all slaves are free" order. Formerly enslaved Texans planned to celebrate their freedom, exactly two years after the Emancipation Proclamation was issued.

A small notice appeared in a local newspaper on December 31, 1865. "All [Black people] residing in Galveston," it read, "are invited to attend on New Year's Morning, at 10 o'clock, at the Public Square, to celebrate the **abolition** of slavery." There was a special call to African Americans in uniform. "United States officers," it stated, "are especially desired to be present."

More than 800 Black men, women, and children turned out for the event. The crowd walked from the Galveston county courthouse to Reedy Chapel Church, where they had gathered on June 19, 1865. There were speakers, a reading of President Lincoln's proclamation, and songs. The 1866 march through Galveston was a long-awaited celebration. They were finally free.

Parents and children stand outside a Freedmen's school on Edisto Island, South Carolina.

Chapter Four

THE JUNETEENTH TRADITION

Newly freed Texans made their way north and west. Some went to the border states of Louisiana, Arkansas, and Oklahoma. Many stayed in Texas. In fact, the state's first majority–African American city wasn't far from Galveston. Independence Heights, now a part of Houston, became an official city in 1915.

In 1866, formerly enslaved people in Galveston and other parts of Texas marked the first Juneteenth. There were prayers, cookouts, and the singing of spirituals, or religious songs. Freedom had been tempered by fear of violence against Blacks. Some gathered quietly.

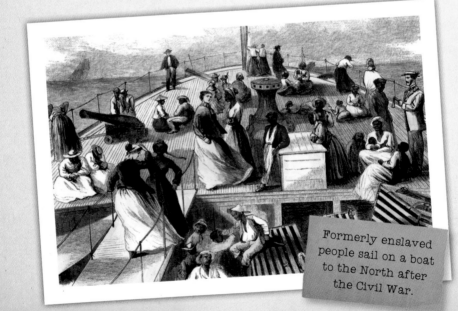

Formerly enslaved people sail on a boat to the North after the Civil War.

People gather outside a Freedmen's Bureau in South Carolina. The U.S. government established these offices to help provide formerly enslaved workers with educational and employment opportunities.

The next year, in 1867, the Freedmen's Bureau helped organize a Texas Juneteenth. The site was a park in Austin, the state capital. That celebration included a prayer service. Songs and dancing followed. Then, the Freedmen's Bureau director read the Emancipation Proclamation. Austin's first Juneteenth became an annual community event.

The first Juneteenths featured baseball, fishing, dancing, music, and storytelling. There were parades, fireworks, horseback riding, and rodeo shows. A religious service with speakers always took place. People dressed in their finest clothing. Clothes were a celebration of newfound freedom.

A band celebrates Juneteenth at an Austin, Texas, park in 1900.

Food, often meager during slavery, was plentiful at Juneteenth celebrations. People set up elaborate barbecue pits. They might roast a pig overnight. Everyone made special dishes to share. There was homemade strawberry lemonade or red soda. The red color of the drink held meaning. It was a tribute to teas made from hibiscus flowers and kola nuts that came to the Americas from West Africa. Some say it recalls blood spilled during slavery or survival through hard times, past and present.

Owning the site where African Americans honored their freedom became an important part of the first Juneteenths. Hosting the day as property owners marked progress from slavery. It also meant Black people did not need permission to gather and celebrate.

In 1872, a group of formerly enslaved Texans raised more than $800 to buy a piece of land. They purchased 10 acres (4 ha) near today's Houston for Juneteenth celebrations. Emancipation Park remains the oldest public park in Texas. The Black community northeast of Waco, Texas, purchased land near Lake Mexia in 1898 for Juneteenth. Booker T. Washington Park was named for the American educator and former slave.

> Emancipation Park in Houston was recognized as an important historic site in Texas. In 2019, the United Nations cultural agency UNESCO honored the Juneteenth site as part of its Slave Route Project.

In time, Juneteenth spread to other parts of the country. The people of Texas took the celebration with them as they **migrated**. Juneteenth appeared in California, Illinois, Florida, and Alabama. Celebrations large and small have taken place all over the United States since then.

This 1939 photo shows a man drinking from a "colored" water cooler in Oklahoma.

The Juneteenth tradition declined during the first half of the 20th century. Perhaps there seemed to be fewer freedoms to celebrate. **Jim Crow laws** were put into place in the South beginning in the 1870s. These laws enforced the separation of the races. Black Americans attended separate, inferior schools. They were forced to sit in the back of public buses. They drank water from separate fountains. Jim Crow laws ended in the 1950s with the **civil rights movement**.

Then came June 19, 1968. Civil rights leader Martin Luther King Jr. had been slain on April 4. Thousands, still mourning King's death, had joined his Poor People's Campaign in Washington, DC. The campaign for economic equality lasted several weeks. It ended with a Juneteenth **Solidarity** Day. That day inspired people to revive the tradition in their home communities. It gave Juneteenth a new importance around the country.

Chapter Five

PROGRESS

From New York to California, Juneteenth has become a day of celebration for Black American families. They share stories rooted in history and take pride in their progress. They gather with family and friends to celebrate being Americans. They hold picnics, barbecue, and grill foods local to their region. They bake strawberry pies and red velvet cake. Fort Worth, Texas, holds a Miss Juneteenth **pageant**, a prayer breakfast, art exhibits, and a road race.

Dancers in Wisconsin celebrating Juneteenth in 2019.

Opal Lee, an activist and Texan, has worked to make Juneteenth a national holiday.

Texas made Juneteenth an official state holiday on January 1, 1980. An African American state legislator named Al Edwards of Houston sponsored the bill. Since then, 46 other states and Washington, DC, have made Juneteenth a state holiday or day of observation.

In 2020, Nike, Target, and Twitter announced plans to observe Juneteenth as a permanent paid holiday.

Many have worked to recognize June 19 as a national holiday. For years, Opal Lee, born in 1926 in Marshall, Texas, has campaigned for Black Independence Day. Every year, Texas Congresswoman Sheila Jackson Lee introduces a resolution to recognize the day's historical importance. In 2020, it had more than 200 other sponsors. She also introduced a bill to make it a federal holiday. John Cornyn of Texas proposed a similar bill in the U.S. Senate.

The events of 2020 sparked new interest in Juneteenth and its history. On May 25, 2020, police killed a Black man named George Floyd in Minneapolis, Minnesota. Mass demonstrations followed during the **COVID-19** outbreak. People marched in support of **Black Lives Matter** to protest violence and injustice against African Americans. Floyd was killed a month before Juneteenth Day 2020 and more than 150 years after General Granger announced "all slaves are free."

Between 15 and 26 million people took part in the 2020 Black Lives Matter protests. Experts say it may be the largest movement in U.S. history.

Juneteenth 2020 included calls for racial justice around the country. New Yorkers, masked to prevent the spread of COVID-19, protested the killing of George Floyd.

"Juneteenth has never been a celebration of victory, or an acceptance of the way things are," said Barack Obama, the first African American president, on June 19, 2020. "It's a celebration of progress. It's an affirmation that despite the most painful parts of our history, change is possible." Juneteenth remains the oldest national celebration of the end of slavery in the United States.

The Juneteenth flag was designed in 1997. It features the red, white, and blue colors of the American flag. The bursting white star represents Texas and new beginnings.

Celebrating Juneteenth and supporting the Black Lives Matter movement in Chicago, Illinois.

**Emancipation Park and Booker T. Washington Park
were both purchased by Black communities.**
Why do you think it was important that early celebrations
of Juneteenth took place on land that they (Black people) owned?

**The Constitution ended slavery in 1865. But then white people
immediately set up Black codes—laws that carried on the conditions
of slavery. Later, Jim Crow laws enforced the separation of races.
These are examples structural racism.**
What are some ways that this racism affects the lives of Black people today?
Can you think of a new example of structural racism?

TIME LINE

1860

1870

1950

1861
The U.S. Civil War begins on April 12.

1863
President Lincoln's Emancipation Proclamation frees enslaved people in the Confederate states, as of January 1.

1865
The U.S. Civil War ends on April 9. Union general Gordon Granger reads his "all slaves are free" order in Galveston, Texas, on June 19. The Thirteenth Amendment outlawing slavery is formally approved on December 6.

1866
Freed Texans celebrate the first anniversary of their emancipation on January 1 in Galveston.

1867
The Freedmen's Bureau helps organize a Juneteenth celebration in Austin, Texas.

1870s
Jim Crow laws are put into place in the South, enforcing separation of the races.

1872
Formerly enslaved Texans buy land for Juneteenth called Emancipation Park in Houston, Texas.

1950s
Jim Crow laws end in the South with the civil rights movement.

**What are some advantages to being white,
both in history and today?**
Explain your answer.

Juneteenth is not yet a federal holiday.
Do you think it should be? Why or why not?

Imagine a world where everyone treated each other better.
Would that solve racism?

1960 **1980** **1990** **2020**

1968
Juneteenth Solidarity
Day is held at the
end of Poor People's
Campaign in
Washington, DC.

1980
Texas makes
Juneteenth an official
state holiday.

1997
Juneteenth.com
tracks celebrations
in the United States
and world.

2020
Bills to make June 19
a federal holiday are
introduced in the U.S.
Congress.

June 19, 1865

abolished (uh-BOL-ishd)
When something has been abolished, it has been outlawed. Slavery was abolished in the United States in 1865.

abolition (ab-uh-LISH-un)
The abolition of slavery means outlawing its practice. Many people, Black and white, celebrated the abolition of slavery.

Black Lives Matter (BLAK LYVZ MAT-tur)
Black Lives Matter is a social movement that was formed in 2013 to fight racism and police violence against African Americans.

civil rights movement (SIV-ull RYTS MOOV-munt)
The civil rights movement refers to the struggle for equal rights for Black Americans in the United States during the 1950s and 1960s.

COVID-19
COVID-19 is a disease that has spread worldwide since 2019. It is short for **co**rona**vi**rus **d**isease 20**19**.

descendant (dee-SEND-unt)
A descendant is a family member in the generations that follow.

economic equality (ek-uh-NOM-ik ee-KWAL-ih-tee)
Economic equality is having the same rights to earn wealth. Black people have long had to struggle for economic equality.

involuntary servitude (in-VOL-un-tayr-ee SERV-ih-tood)
Involuntary servitude is forcing a person to be enslaved to another.

Jim Crow laws
These laws enforced separation of the races in the South. They lasted from the 1870s through the 1950s. Jim Crow was a character demeaning to Black people in a stage performance that began in 1828.

migrated (MY-gray-ted)
When people migrate, they move from one place to another. Juneteenth celebrations spread as people migrated to new areas.

pageant (PAJ-unht)
A pageant is a public show in which people walk in processions or act out historical scenes. Fort Worth, Texas holds a Miss Juneteenth pageant.

racial discrimination (RAY-shull diss-krim-ih-NAY-shun)
Racial discrimination is unfair treatment of people based on their race. Racial discrimination comes in many forms.

solidarity (sahl-uh-DAYR-ih-tee)
Solidarity means unity based on common goals.

BOOKS

Adamson, Thomas K. *The Civil War*. Mankato, MN: The Child's World, 2015.

Cooper, Floyd. *Juneteenth for Mazie*. Fairfax, VA: Library Ideas, 2019.

Grack, Rachel. *Juneteenth*. Minneapolis, MN: Bellwether Media, 2018.

Johnson, Angela. *All Different Now: Juneteenth, the First Day of Freedom*. New York, NY: Simon & Schuster Books for Young Readers, 2014.

Nelson, Vaunda Micheaux. *Juneteenth*. Minneapolis, MN: Millbrook Press, 2006.

Reader, Jack. *The Story Behind Juneteenth*. New York, NY: PowerKids Press, 2020.

WEBSITES

Visit our website for links about Juneteenth:

childsworld.com/links

Note to Parents, Teachers, and Librarians: We routinely verify our Web links to make sure they are safe, active sites—so encourage your readers to check them out!

INDEX